THE WISDOM OF THE ORACLE

(Inspiring Messages of the Soul)

By Dr. John F. Demartini

Edited by Matthew

ISBN: 0-75962-022-9

This book is printed on acid free paper.

1stBooks - rev. 6/4/01

FOREWORD

Certain gifted writers have the ability to open up the doorway to the Soul and to share their wondrous insights in immortal works such as "The Prophet" by Kahlil Gibran or James Allen's perennial classic "As A Man Thinketh".

Now a new Soul experience is available. This new book *The Wisdom of the Oracle* (the result of inspired meditation and experience) opens up the doorway to the heart and the soul. A rare jewel of inspired writing, *The Wisdom of the Oracle* offers profound insights into our earthly and spiritual powers. It reveals the practical and the enlightened way to overcome the troubles and complexities of everyday life.

TABLE OF CONTENTS

INTRODUCTION

"We can sometimes escape from jail, but we cannot escape from our thoughts. Unwise thinking is the key to imprisonment, and wise thinking is the key to freedom. Thought is the key, which locks or opens all the doors of Life. Dominant thoughts select which doors we choose to open. Shall we visit heaven or hell today?"

Does the way we think effect our health, relationships, career, sense of self-worth, our everyday reality and our future potential? The author of *The Wisdom of the Oracle*, Dr. John Demartini is convinced that when we fail to listen to our Soul and think our highest Soul-connected thoughts, we fall prey to our lower earthly senses - and when we listen to our ground-bound senses we immediately and completely lose our way upon the pathway of life, love and light.

This poetic and magnificent book is written from the heart and soul levels of life's operation. Its concepts and insights offer the reader jewels of inspiration and its soul message is clear, concise and timely in this highly technological and super pressured era.

The Wisdom of the Oracle combines human and spiritual insights with scientific methods. While spiritually connecting the reader to the Soul, it is also based on solid, basic practical everyday type reasoning.

This book will awaken you to a new level of awareness and inspire you into taking definite action. It will reveal how your Life is like a movie screen reflecting whatever you project upon it with your thoughts. Every loving dream, every loving wish is possible when you listen to the wisdom of your inner oracle.

Reading *The Wisdom of the Oracle* reminds you of your Life's purpose. It will cheer, uplift and reawaken you to your own highest Soul potential...because you are also the *Oracle*.

I

AS A MAN THINKETH
IN HIS HEART SO IS HE

We cannot see our thoughts, but we can experience the sum total of their results, in the form of personal habits. Imagine a tape-recording in which each track is recorded, layer over layer, without erasing the tape first. After many layers, the final product could be noise, or beautiful music, depending on the skill and intent of the producer. Over time, every one of our new thoughts combines with all previous thoughts to strengthen or weaken the foundation upon which our Life is built.

Effectively, our human character is the summation of all our thoughts and in turn, our habits. Every thought, habit, or behavior builds our character, brick by brick. Habits are thoughts applied over time to form predictable patterns in our physical, emotional, mental, or spiritual structures. Each thought has an opportunity to forge the first link in a new chain of habit, or to follow established paths carved in the rock of our past existence, as the river follows its own riverbed.

The very term "human," is derived from the combination of the two root words "humus" and "mana." Humus means *earthly*, organic soil, and mana means *mind*, light or intelligence. When our *mind* attunes to our *earthly* form, we learn to physically express our thoughts. Our most dominant thoughts quickly become our habitual reactions and the development of our character traits soon follow.

If we volunteer to control our thoughts from inside, and our sensory perceptions (such as vision and hearing) from outside, we forge new chains of habit, encouraging character in the direction we wish it to grow. If we see beauty and hear beauty, we tend to think beauty and speak beauty. This is how we learn to express a more beautiful character.

Every one of our mind's thoughts is influenced by a host of external bodily sensations including sights, sounds, tastes, smells and feelings. Each present thought, combines with a turbulent internal stream of past sensory experiences, known as "memories." Combined, they give rise to another winding river of future "imaginations." If we attune primarily to our physical bodily senses, we become the sum and total of these denser physical, earthly thoughts. If we attune to the higher light of our Soul, we develop a lighter, more evolved state of character, and we invoke a higher state of mind. True genius appears spontaneously from this realm of thought. It is beautifully expressed, when our character aligns powerfully with the forces of Divine inspiration. Suddenly the Divine creation becomes creative, the beautiful scenery becomes the seer and our true character becomes Divine.

Dr. John F. Demartini

If we attune to the higher light of our Soul, we develop a lighter, more evolved state of character, and we invoke a higher state of mind. True genius appears spontaneously from this realm of thought.

4

II

SEED AND PLANT

The fruits of our labor arise from the seeds of our thought. Little effort need be put forth to grow weeds, but constant attention is required to cultivate an orderly and productive garden. As we sow, so shall we reap. Our mighty dreams are first conceived by our higher inspired minds. Then these very elevated thoughts become things. As we believe, so we achieve. Our mind can express either the creations of our true higher being or the more lowly, illusive thoughts of our personas.

Our personas, or who we temporarily think we are, are the essential and ever-changing parts of our mind's earthly experience. These changing selves are always balanced fluidly and perfectly, like the two ends of a seesaw. Our personas are expressed as positive and negative, pleasure and pain, joy and sorrow. They may be conscious or unconscious. Our personas shift like sand in the desert and it is hard to build the house of our lives on their sand.

Fortunately, a mysterious realm of mind exists above and beyond this fragile bubble of Earth. Philosophers and theologians call it "Soul." When our thoughts and deeds rise to the level of our Soul we become one with a greater reality. We are freed from the troublesome confusion of our earthly existence. It is only from this realm that our thoughts are inspired in Love.

If we listen to the tales of our physical senses (as most of us do), we become fragmented into our personas, which are the two-faced theater masks, one side smiling, and one side frowning. Which mask shall we wear today? This is a ready source of our temporary excitement, throwing off sparks of passion and emotion at every turn. Of course, sparks might also burn the house down. But, eventually we come to unconditional state, when we give birth to, or partake of a genuine Love through the voice of our Soul. Our passions are created through our personas. Our true Love is created through our Soul.

The seed of every thought transmits its essence to the fall harvest. If dominant thoughts of elation and depression, or joy and sorrow, rule our pasture, then human "mortality" is produced. Mortality is harvested from sowing the two-faced mask of dualism. This mortality misaligns our true nature; it gives us lopsidedness, and other signs of imbalance. On the other hand, if we plant in alignment the Soulful seeds of Love in our gardens, we will reap the immortal thoughts of genius, thoughts full of balance and beauty, all integrated into a new seed of Love.

On the other hand, if we plant in alignment the Soulful seeds of Love in our gardens, we will reap the immortal thoughts of genius, thoughts full of balance and beauty, all integrated into a new seed of Love.

III

GOOD AND EVIL

"Good" and "evil" are subjective measures of the same loving mind substance, much as electricity, having no will of its own, serving its master. We can use electrical power to bestow the death sentence or light the world. Wisdom and Love determine our sensible use of all mental or electrical power.

Lopsided thoughts, shrouded in darkness, tend toward emotional imbalance. Loving thoughts spontaneously emit the balance of clarity, purity and truth. Good and evil thoughts are lopsided perceptions of what is, clothed in the dust of dishonor, attempting to block the light of our true balanced magnificence. A pure thought is perfectly shaped and clear, through which lens we can see the glory of our creation. We are given the power of a liberated will, to choose either the seeds of our physical illusions, or the truth expressed by our Soul.

Good and evil thoughts are the cause of the cyclic emotions of joy and sorrow, happiness and sadness. True thought, pure thought, is the very essence and initiator of Love and Gratitude to the perfect Creator, and a thanksgiving for our own perfection. How could it be otherwise?

IV

THOUGHT

The stronger our thoughts become, the more surely they take form in our lives. A beast spends its waking moments in search of basic needs such as food; we too are drawn to the level of the beast through our hungers, fears, and desires of gratification of the physical senses. But our thoughts of Soul are different. They enter by a narrow gate into our Heart with Love. Our Soul's voice guides us to angelic realms, where genius and beauty flow abundantly. Thoughts can align us downward with the beast, to inevitable decay and death of our physical form; or lift us up in the hands of God.

A God-like thought is indeed the thought of God. It reflects truth, purity, divine design, as our moon mirrors the lighted fire of our Sun. Our mind in form takes shape and evolves through spiritual growth. The acorn in its single-minded persistence becomes a tall oak tree, seeking greater Light. May our thoughts ascend from beast to Heaven.

Our Soul's voice guides us to angelic realms, where genius and beauty flow abundantly.

V

WEAPONS OR TOOLS

The light of our Soul, or our mental "mana," connects us directly with the Divine and Infinite Intelligence through "our golden ray." Our mind's earthly connection, the "humus," anchors us to our more beastly nature. Our Soul reflects unity, while our human senses reflect duality. In the field of duality, two choices must always exist, else the playing field itself would simply disappear: good/bad, here/there, up/down, hot/cold, joy/sorrow. These choices are always based in illusion, in the polarization of positive and negative. Our earthly mind bows its head toward God, but where is God not?

Our infinite Soul brings balance to our perceptions; it brightens our heart flame with Love, Wisdom, and Power. Our Soul directs our personal valor and it befits us as a cherished entity originally created in the image of God. A musical choir has many voices, each tuned to its own task and rung of achievement, yet all may sing in harmony from low to high for a mutual reward. Humble submission to our greater Master uplifts all. To listen for and obey that wisdom of Divine perfection is Truth and Genius in action. To speak of and know true Love is the essence of true worth.

Our infinite Soul brings balance to our perceptions; it brightens our heart flame with Love, Wisdom, and Power.

VI

MASTER OF THOUGHT, CHARACTER AND DESTINY

A child proves to itself that it exists, literally through its own physical movement. If the child ceases to move, it ceases to exist, at least from its own point of view. Similarly, the Mind proves its existence by thinking; it thinks, therefore, it is. Mental thoughts become material things, and the thoughts of God become the expressed light images of God.

If we limit ourselves simply to being mortal, our earthly ego attempts to reign over all it surveys. We want to be king of the jungle. As we un-limit ourselves toward the Immortal, our mental potential expands. We become both the creation and the creative, through expression and Divine inspiration. At this stage, we transcend the illusive world of our ego.

But rest assured that our ego will not give over its power without a fight, just as the child does not give up its toys or other imagined possessions gladly. Paradoxically, it is at this very edge of chaos and destruction where maximum evolution and true construction begin. We either learn or experience the consequences.

It is impossible to build without destroying, and equally impossible to destroy without building. These acts are interchangeable, and merely transform that which is indestructible from one shape to another. The phoenix rises from the ashes; and both are constructed of the same atoms.

If we seek to cultivate a garden, we "build" a crop. This crop may be intentionally "destroyed" and plowed under, but the field itself becomes equally fertile simultaneously. We have neither created nor destroyed anything. We have merely transformed one form of energy and matter into another.

This simple plan extends to every level of consciousness, from finite to infinite. We may tune in at the ground level and see desolation and barren land or we may look above such shallow appearances and discover in all manner the many fertile opportunities, which spring forth. Las Vegas was built in a desert, and Florida grew from a swamp. All we have to do is understand and appreciate the Divine system of balance.

We have the capacity to benefit from each transition point, where the sand greets the sea; for we as man or woman, are the masters of our fate, and the captains of our Souls. God provides the wind in our sails, but we are certainly allowed to hold the rudder.

God provides the wind in our sails, but we are certainly allowed to hold the rudder.

VII

FOOLISHNESS AND WISDOM

Every condition, which originates from our earthly anchored mind, is subjective, opinionated and dualistic. Though it still gives us the freedom to choose wisely, and thereby increase our storehouse of wisdom, all earthly derived conditions must have their polar opposites. Positive cannot be without negative, and negative perpetually is drawn to its positive mate, so their collective charges can balance. Every joy has its sorrow and every sorrow has its joy. Pregnancy depletes the mother-host of certain organic substances (destruction), but gives form to the baby (construction).

If we manage to rise above our local illusions of any imbalance and look from a greater elevation, we see a grander scheme of order. A short airplane trip above the clouds would serve to illustrate this point. Our perspective from a higher place allows us to visualize the checkerboards of farmland, the arteries of metropolis, the grace and grandeur of Nature. The higher balance and order of our bigger picture represents a more efficient reflection than the lower and imbalanced chaos of our little view.

So it is with every condition. When we are wise, we will reflect upon our local illusions, discover their inherent opposites, and study the lesson stored within their condition, until our wisdom unfolds. Pursuit of excellence develops balanced character, and strengthens our mastery over the seeming inconsistencies of day-to-day life. It is our choice to be slaves of condition, like a leaf in the wind with a mouth; or to master the outer world through the inner voice, where Divine Order, balance and harmony measure all events with their own larger scale of perfection.

VIII

CAUSE AND EFFECT

This Universe runs upon a magnificent framework of "cause" and "effect." Any given cause or event will result in a predictable and equal effect or result. There is no random behavior in an orderly Universe, only a bouquet of possibilities. Quantum chaos is order yet to be awakened.

As mortals, we experience a statistically significant amount of physical cellular mortality, known as the aging process. This process starts at birth, and pursues its inevitable course to death. In between, some of us get old, while others simply get older. Our age itself is not what is significant, but rather the importance we attach to it. At certain times, a trial of "dis-ease" may appear to test us, usually followed by a "cure." Both are but lessons of Love.

The healing arts and sciences often search for the causes of diseases; but if we examine the diseases themselves and their underlying causes, we realize they are one and the same.

In an orderly Universe, no therapy is complete until cause equals effect in space - time. When the lesson concerning the cause of the disease is learned, the cure is immediate and absolute.

The quality of our future depends upon our present thoughts, in a cause and effect relationship. There is no sin, but a misunderstanding and no punishment, but a consequence. We recognize that thoughts affect our emotional, mental, and spiritual states. Thoughts are powerful tools in our physical being, for ordering or disordering. Ultimately, thought is the cause, and life itself is the effect.

Our outer world has its victims, while our inner Soul has its victory. We seek freedom from anger, fear and guilt, but this peace of mind is obtained only through the message of our Soul. Our Soul's message maintains that all is Love, yet all is law. If we attempt to avoid our lessons of Love, law dictates that we repeat those lessons until we pass Love's course. School is the same everywhere! What we fear comes near, and what we flee begins to follow us. What we follow, flees, and what we love, we live, until we are moved to transcend beyond it.

Whatever we condemn, we create, attract, or become until we love. This is again the law of cause and effect, in space - time. Upon self-mastery we understand and use this principle to our advantage. As masters we alter our minds and thoughts, and thereby cause alterations in our environment or reality and our lives begin to change. This is because our inner Soul rules and not our outer world. Now we are masters of cause and effect.

IX

THE GARDEN

Our minds are fertile Gardens of Eden, ready at command to produce golden sunflowers. But the serpent is always poised, eager to distract. We are wise to plant scriptures of Love and Gratitude for our Creator; else the weeds of illusion dull our senses, take root, entangle us needlessly, and block the radiance of our Souls so completely that growth beneath the darkness becomes almost impossible. This debilitating condition is combated with Gratitude in words of Wisdom and Love. The radiance of God always reveals the flower to us again. Its seed has never left our garden, but, if we do not plant flowers in our gardens, we will forever pull weeds.

We may passively allow the weeds of illusion to fill every space in our plot; or we can actively choose to harvest, through Grace, our Soul's truth of Love and Gratitude to our Creator. If we hear only the voice of our Soul, and see only the vision of our Soul, then our reward flows effortlessly and abundantly from our harmonious Universe. May we cultivate our flowers,

25

nourish them with Love, have Gratitude and Humility toward God, and may all universal secrets unfold like petals of the lotus, one by one. The seed is always inside the fruit.

If we hear only the voice of our Soul, and see only the vision of our Soul, then our reward flows effortlessly and abundantly from our harmonious Universe.

X

INNER THOUGHT AND
OUTER CONDITION

All existence is based on two components, Sound and Light. "And God Said, 'Let there be Light, and there was Light'." Every one of us resonates on a specific and unique frequency or "fingerprint" of Sound and Light, just as each crystal or musical instrument has its very own individual tone and hue. Whatever this frequency, circumstances are attracted to us which harmonize with it. Like attracts like; water seeks its own level. If we fear, then a disharmony of fear is brought forth, until we learn to change our tune, for such is the order and freedom of the Universe. If we Love, then Heaven's own choir sings with us.

Several old-fashioned cuckoo clocks can be placed on a wall, with their pendulums swinging at different rates. Within a day, all the pendulums will swing together in unison. A tuning fork, which is struck and then held near the strings of a guitar, will cause the guitar to hum along. This is the law of harmonic vibration. Humanity itself marches in armies to the beat of whatever distant drummer is most attractive at the moment. Even our Universe has rhythm; just ask the stars.

Our mind is continuously reflecting lightness and darkness, generating a symphony or cacophony of our dominant thoughts. Imbalanced dominant thoughts produce an unappealing disharmony called "noise." A room full of quiet children is improbable at best, unless the teacher is there to guide them. Adults generate a more sophisticated, more practiced brand of noise. If at some point a strong and dominating desire arises for a person, place, or thing (called an infatuation), a pattern arises in which later infatuations and inevitable resentments dominate otherwise sensible behavior. Witness today's modern newlyweds, each on their third marriage, while the band plays "Love is a Many-Splendored Thing."

If we focus on poverty, then poverty calls for the song of further poverty, to support our illusion of that vision. What we fear comes near, because we strengthen our focus on that thought. If we loosen the bonds of fear, concentrating instead on Love, the opposite occurs: a focus point of wealth, material or spiritual, resonates with the Universal law of mental precipitation. Nothing succeeds like success; and banks are always happy to lend money to people who have plenty of it. We ourselves choose what will enter our lives, as victim or Victor, consciously or unconsciously, according to our needs, wants, desires and loves.

It is our destiny to recognize our Creator, and the creativity endowed within us. We become Masters of Life insofar as we demonstrate our understanding of Love, Wisdom, Power, Grace, Humility, and Gratitude. Our mind is purified, drop-by-drop, as we learn to edit our dominant thoughts, eliminating dense and cloudy obfuscation, and listening to clear messages of our Soul, with its music of the spheres and harmony of the angels. We are guided by our Soul upward, outward to the Light and Sound of God. For it is commanded, "They who have eyes, let them see, and they who have ears, let them hear."

We are guided by our Soul upward, outward to the Light and Sound of God.

XI

CHANCE OR CHOICE

"Evolution" unfolds in two ways, by outward expansion and inward contraction. We evolve in both directions simultaneously. Breathing in and breathing out are both necessary to sustain our evolving life.

This evolution becomes expressed in the form of concentric rings, moving inward like rings on an archery target as we aim closer to the purposeful center to hit the bulls eye. Yet this evolution also ripples outward, like the rings of water on a pond when a pebble is dropped into it. As we boldly go where we have not been before, we earn promotions to greater concentric rings or spheres of influence. Our responsibility, and reward, like in any well-run business, though, continues to grow. This outward progression is infinite; but at any stage we can also reverse the waves on the pond, and move inward to the center bull's eye, to that single point called Unity. It is this central point, which further guides our evolution along. Ultimately, all Being expands toward greater Light, and simultaneously returns to the One for nourishment. Our Sun is most dark and dense at its core, and most brilliant and ethereal on its surface, yet all energy remains in perfect balance. Balance is the key.

We choose the events of our lives. Even choosing not to choose is itself a choice, earning only the pyrrhic luxury of being a "victim" to outside circumstance or victor of the inner world. Every choice has a consequence, as every cause has its effect.

Each circumstance may be likened to a stone, used either to build upon, or weigh us down. As the river cuts its way inexorably through the hardest rock, we may dissolve any stone through the universal solvent of Love and Gratitude.

Every time we practice our Love and Gratitude with Humility, we are permitted to evolve to a greater sphere. Each time we choose, so-called rightly or wrongly, we dictate our own boundaries by the resulting circumstances of that choice. If we think imbalance, then our lives become a lopsided reflection of that imbalance, just as our eyes see a blurred world if the eye muscles are out of balance. If we consciously practice our search for balance, as we might exercise our eye muscles to bring vision into better focus, we learn to see through the eyes of Love and Gratitude for all circumstances.

33

Wisdom and growth occur at such moments. Our Soul places no limits upon us...we choose our own fences. May we become centered and poised for our infinite expansion.

Each circumstance may be likened to a stone, used either to build upon, or weigh us down.

XII

LITTLE CHILDREN

We definitely take a step closer to Heaven, when we awaken from the illusion of blaming others for the discomforts of our own life. Society presently finds ample reward in its fashionable "victim mentality." How much easier it is to deny personal responsibility, to say, "The Devil / bad childhood / friends / television / genetics / rock music made me do it!" Granted, these pervasive influences are often not easy to transcend; but we still can control our perceptions or thoughts. Astonishingly, the same "bad" life could just as easily be interpreted, by a more enlightened viewer, as Heaven on Earth. "One man's food is another man's poison."

Our anger, fear and guilt separate us, like barbed wire, from a cascade of natural Beauty surrounding us. A walk in Nature helps to remove this sense of isolation. We become unified, through Love and Gratitude, with the Grace of God. Our magnificent Universe recites volumes to us, fills our eyes with radiant images, and lifts us to higher planes.

Little children close their eyes, and in darkness imagine themselves powerful because the stars disappear. May we open our eyes and come to know the beauty that's true.

Our magnificent Universe recites volumes to us, fills our eyes with radiant images, and lifts us to higher planes.

XIII

FALL AND RISE

We are stubborn creatures. If we refuse to learn in bliss, we most certainly will learn by amiss. Each trial is a potential stepping-stone to greatness, just as passing each test in school allows a student to graduate to more difficult grades, with increasing rewards for each success. Logically, the student then becomes the teacher for those below, as these lessons are mastered. A truly great Teacher serves with Love, Gratitude, and Humility toward past Masters who have gone before, paving the way, building bridges for future generations. In the stream of Life, an outstretched hand is often enough to help one to the other side. The teacher takes neither credit nor blame for lessons offered; for indeed there is nothing new under the Sun. Gladness of heart is its own reward, for it lets us know we can help guide another in their upward quest toward freedom.

Nature always fills a vacuum. Our minds will eagerly fill an empty space, either with treasures or trash, just as quickly as we fill the empty closets of a new house. Our upward spiral of evolution rides the wings of Love. The curriculum of our Evolution University teaches Love as the steps of our Stairway to Heaven, for some of us fly, while others choose to walk. Whatever the means of transportation, we cannot take the next step up until we learn to Love our present step unconditionally. Simply put, if we do not Love something, we continue to attract its lesson into our lives until we do Love it. Each meeting of this lesson is an opportunity to interpret it, analyze it, search for its hidden blessing, "Get it right this time," and learn it, so that we can graduate to the next grade. Our lesson is always Love.

One useful truth of the Universe is that we are never presented with a problem unless we can solve it, either by ourselves or with the help of others. An orderly Universe does not hand a child struggling with addition and subtraction a complex problem in calculus, and demand that the child answer its riddle; this privilege is earned, step-by-step. Our Soul continuously makes the necessary tools and skills available to complete the job, and indeed there are really no problems, only opportunities to learn another lesson in Love. As a wise student, may we welcome our experiences bearing the appearance of adversity, for each imaginary barrier is a personal challenge to grow. Fitness training requires us to climb ropes and jump fences. May our minds become fit.

With growth comes a greater concentric sphere of influence, responsibility, and reward. We gradually discover who we are. We discover that we are a Divine expression of our Soul, a Light of God, a Being of magnificence and beauty.

As we travel through Life and take on the challenges of difficult experiences, Love dissolves these circumstances, and gives us greater strength. Kahlil Gibran: "Love grinds us to whiteness, kneads us until we are pliant, then assigns us to God's sacred fire, that we may become sacred bread for God's sacred feast."

We gradually discover who we are. We discover that we are a Divine expression of our Soul, a Light of God, a Being of magnificence and beauty.

XIV

ROOT AND FRUIT

Pain has the lesson of pleasure at its core, and pleasure also speaks intimately of pain. One cannot exist without the other, just as "hot" cannot be without "cold." All is relative on this earthly plane of illusion. How we interpret each lesson is defined by our thoughts and past experiences, much like computer software defines a servant machine's response to its master's keyboard input. Change the software and you change the response. A person who has not eaten for a day may feel starved, while another who has purposely fasted for three days may seek religious ecstasy. The body feels the same, but the mind set is different.

Genuine Love is birthed from this experience of both sides. Evolution is halted if we deny either side its moment in our lives, and emotional growth, maturity, and wisdom blossom forth when we embrace all lessons with equal anticipation. This is the gift of our Creator: experiences of pain and pleasure teach us Love.

Chance favors the prepared mind. Temporary selective attention to either pain or pleasure, through the illusive senses, will also eventually teach its opposite side. We then obtain the great true worth of understanding both sides of Life. How else could the rich man understand poverty?

This is the gift of our Creator: experiences of pain and pleasure teach us Love.

XV

DOMINANT THOUGHT

Our private and public experiences enter our lives through the gate of our "Dominant Thought," even though this connection may be invisible to us. The Law of Momentum dictates that an object pushed in one direction continues in that direction with increasing speed and force. A car stalled in the road may require two strong adults to get it moving; but once it is rolling along, even a small child can push with equal effectiveness. The same is true of thought, the more persistent a thought over time, the stronger its influence from minute-to-minute, day-to-day, and year-to-year. Our dominant thought literally becomes who we are.

One of our greatest freedoms is the freedom of thought. Fortunately, technology has made remarkable advances, but it still cannot hear what we are thinking. We alone control our perception of the grand illusion. There is a price to be paid for this freedom, as with all things, for the price of freedom is eternal vigilance. Throughout history and to the present day, great effort is expended to affect our thinking processes; for example, "Buy this, vote for that, look like such, do this and you will be happy," or similar variations. Oddly, the promise is always shallow and unfulfilling once we attain its supposed benefit, leaving another hunger in its place, for balance is <u>not</u> part of this formula. The beginning of genuine freedom comes from asking two questions: what would I love; and why would I love it? If our answer to any strong desire has its roots in the equation of Love and Gratitude with Humility, then seeds of permanent fulfillment have been planted effectively.

Wisdom takes perception and links it to purpose. Foolishness believes that the outside world is not linked to the inside world. But the emperor's clothes are transparent to the mirror of Life. Wisdom knows that our past thoughts are our present experiences; and our present thoughts are our future experiences. This is reassuring, for no one is condemned by the grim past to a future of misery. When we finally see cause and effect as one, we transcend thoughts of separation from our Creator, and birth "present-time-consciousness." We atone for our past "illusions" and become at-one with the presence of God.

Wisdom takes perception and links it to purpose.

XVI

ATTRACTION

We can sometimes escape from jail; but we cannot escape from our thoughts. Unwise thinking is the key to imprisonment, and wise thinking is the key to freedom. Thought is the key, which locks or opens all the doors of Life. Dominant thoughts select which doors we choose to open. Shall we visit heaven or hell today?

Thought is a fickle foundation; if cracked or unstable, nothing of substance can stand for long upon it, no matter how elegant the structure we build above it through our illusion. We attract people, places, and events into our lives by the polarity of our thinking, just as surely as the north pole of a magnet attracts south. Crime, poverty, war, destruction, and disease, all are attracted to those thoughts, which encourage and empower them. This attraction may be on a personal level, as a group or even a nation. We can attempt to lock up or even kill an enemy, but ten more wait eagerly outside the castle door. The war of duality always obliges our hidden desires, until we declare the balance of inner peace.

The outer world is a reflection of the inner world. The outer world is a mirror, which Life holds in front of us, that we can see ourselves the way others see us. A painted face is temporary at best. But when our dominant thoughts change, the outer world also changes automatically, for it reflects the essence of our new state of mind.

No society can ever breed laws and justice systems greater than the wisdom of its collective Soul. Illusion grows illusion, and Love grows Love. We reap what we sow.

No society can ever breed laws and justice systems greater than the wisdom of its collective Soul.

XVII

PRICE AND PRIZE

Every growth has its decay; every gain has its loss. Water in a pond must circulate, or else it becomes stagnant and Life within it dies. Resources such as money wither when hoarded, and flourish with a life of their own when they are in constant motion. This is the law of universal balance and perpetual motion. As we share with others, our own riches multiply. Love is ours when we give it away. There is no such thing as something for nothing. Everything has a price, even if the tag is not always attached. All is Love, yet all is Law. Maturity recognizes the pain, the sacrifice necessary to achieve the pleasure of a given purpose. You have to be hungry before you can enjoy your next meal.

Listen to Soul and obey it. Accept the wisdom of pain and pleasure equally in pursuit of your mission and purpose. A Master does this, and is readily willing to pay the same price for either illusion of suffering or joy, with the certain knowledge of a higher reward: fulfillment and expression of Life, Spirit in form, ascension to that vision revealed by angels, purification of Heart through Love.

XVIII

POVERTY

Energy can be neither created nor destroyed. It can only be changed from one vibrational form to another. For example, electricity becomes heat in the filament of a lamp, which in turn radiates light, so electricity is light. But the quantity of energy remains constant. A glass of water may be turned into either ice or steam, but in the end one glass of water, not two, remains.

Our consciousness attracts and perpetuates that which we believe. A belief system based in poverty "knows" the futility of attempting to rise above its own hunger, remaining petty and mean. A belief in universal abundance "knows" riches beyond mortal compre-hension. A single ear of corn contains enough kernels to plant an entire field. They, who have ears, let them hear.

May we finally realize that no matter what we get, it is because of what we give. If we want more, we must give more. The greatest gift is Love, with service performed in the spirit of

Love. Love is inspired by Soul; service is guided by Soul. A wise service done from an inspired motive is permeated with an essential power, which comes from the Heart of love. The result is increased correspondingly. Inspired service automatically receives abundance, recognition, and acceptance. Its example inspires others toward wise thinking.

We cannot fool anyone except ourselves by imagining otherwise. True balance demands that all books balance on the bottom line. All the earthly resources we came into this world with or earned during our lifetime will remain when we leave.

Every diamond Cleopatra wore is still on the planet. Horses do not come adorned with a saddle. Whatever "it" is - we are not going to take "it" with us.

Understanding this, state: "What can I give now, so I may now receive? If I desire something, what price will I pay and how will I do it? I will go and learn from those who have already accomplished, and unless I am willing to do whatever it takes to do so, I do not expect to receive the things that I love. As I sow, so shall I reap."

XIX

PROSPERITY

There is no such thing as something for nothing. We get what we give. We may take from others in our ignorance, not realizing that we are only depleting our own storehouse. Money, like blood, must circulate to remain alive, to retain its vital spark. Generosity for the wise reason is always rewarded in mysterious ways through Universal Law. The shape of coins will change with the realm; but like energy, the abundance they represent can neither be created nor destroyed. Their essence possesses intrinsic beauty and purity, like fine gold or brilliant gems. So too is the essence of our deeds. Definiteness of purpose with wise action will help focus this energy of abundance. A magnifying glass intensifies mild sunlight to blazing heat. Focus is the key.

The message is very simple and very clear: if we do not balance our books, the Universe will do it for us. For example, if an employer lessens the worth of employees, the entire business is cheapened, for good employees are valuable assets.

Both employer and employee must understand that our Universe does not permit something for nothing.

In truth, there is no separation between self and other, or self and Universe. A single drop of seawater possesses all the content and quality of the ocean, without needing to be the ocean. The trick to getting along with other people is to let them be who they are, instead of trying to change them to whom we are. When we give of ourselves and see ourselves as universal, we acknowledge a universal expression through Divinity. Every gift of Love moves from the finite to the infinite, like water rising from the sea to the clouds, and back again to the finite in drops of rain.

The number "0" represents the way of all cycles in the Universe, and the balancing of all books. Everything we send out will return in its own cycle if we are patient. Remember that we cannot force rain from the clouds, when the clouds are ready, the prosperous rains will come.

Prosperity does not always arise from counting arbitrary units of wealth in time and space. True prosperity is the inevitable reward for a willingness to walk the path of service with Love, to open our hearts to the magnificence of our Universe. Prosperity is the fulfillment of void and inner peace of mind. There is nothing gained, nothing lost in the perfect balance of our universe. Love is all there is. This is the true gift of God. When we permit ourselves to Love, we walk in courage. We live by the virtues of Life. We have prosperity.

True prosperity is the inevitable reward for a willingness to walk the path of service with Love, to open our hearts to the magnificence of our Universe.

XX

DISEASE AND HEALTH

A healthy lifestyle incorporates a philosophy of moderation or temperance in all things. Any perceived excess generates imbalance, with a resulting stress upon the system as a whole. Excessive eating, worry, stimulation or sloth will cause 'defects' in our body structure. "Dis-ease" itself is a process of too much and too little, function out of time with need, like a tire out of balance that wobbles as it spins. The light of our Soul is above such influence. Our heart wishes only to guide our life with temperance, if we allow it. Pure balance allows pure motion, with minimum friction and maximum vitality. True balance allows Divinity to express pure genius.

Temperance is the desire of our Soul to flow effortlessly into masterpiece, an intense merging of mortal and Immortal. The secret of a blessed Life is to allow temperance to be our Guide. If the physical senses reign, "too much" and "too little" is usually the result. A thermostat, which is too close to a heating and cooling vent will react with opposite wild blasts of too much heat and too much cold, in a perpetual neurotic attempt to reach balance. The only 'cure' is to recognize the cause and adjust it.

Passion is another manifestation of the physical senses. We often mistake passion for Love, basing our belief in the latest song, movie, romance novel, or popular couple for the moment. But passion is a wild horse galloping at full speed through a forest of experience, exciting but illusive and dangerous. Love is a continuous learning process, starting before birth and growing throughout Life. Love is the sum of many years and many lives. Love brings with it stability, prudence, wisdom, courage, temperance, and abundance. Love is its own reward.

Dr. John F. Demartini

True balance allows Divinity to express pure genius.

XXI

TRUTH

Nothing of our physical senses can ever fully satisfy our Soul. No part of reasoning from our "sensible" earthly mind will ever know the true inspiration and guidance from our Soul. May we be humble and listen to that still, small voice from within, whose whisper is more powerful than all the shouting of this turbulent outer world. "I would rather have the whole world against me than my own Soul", says the wise one.

We cannot fathom the depth of our Soul, from whence springs inspiration and intuition, any more readily than we can see the bottom of the ocean. We must actively seek those rare moments of clarity, when time and place cooperate to give us a glimpse of Truth, as a diver may see treasure on the ocean floor. Our Soul often leads us to doorways of perception, as if to prove they do exist. There are two kinds of people: those who are searching for the Truth of God, and those who through their Soul, have found this Truth Divine.

63

There are two kinds of people: those who are searching for the Truth of God, and those who through their Soul, have found this Truth Divine.

XXII

REAL LIFE

John shares this story: "When I was fourteen years old, I hitchhiked from Houston Texas, through El Paso, on my way to California. During this journey I had the wonderful experience of meeting a bum on the street, who took me into the El Paso library, sat me before a table, put my hands on the books of Aristotle and Plato and told me two great truths. He said, "Young man, I want you to learn two things. Never forget these two things. One is: never judge a book by its cover. Two is: learn how to read. For Wisdom is the only thing that no one can take away". He further said, "The cover will fool you young man. For though you might think I am an old bum, in all truth I am actually a very wealthy man".

The outer superficial covers, which are the crusts, will eventually break, and we will eventually discover the hidden core. The crust will fool us and change like the plate tectonics of our planet's surface geology. The secret is to not let these superficial perceptions of pain and pleasure, or happy and sad, or wealth and poverty, lead us to think that they are true. For the truth is that all of us are One.

We are always what we see in others. We are all an expression of all things. May we let not these temporary, mortal misperceptions rule the true nature of ourselves, or others. When we see our true nature, let us realize that there is nothing but Divine Being, in a Divine habitat, living a Divine Life. When we learn that, we will express our own Divinity. Let not the superficial illusions interfere with the deep truth. Let not the chaos of the outer world interfere with the truth and hidden world of Divine order. Let not the imbalance interfere with the balance. When we discover this truth, we will not react to people. We will instead act with purpose. We are to give our Love to all people.

Let not the chaos of the outer world interfere with the truth and hidden world of Divine order.

XXIII

PAIN AND PLEASURE

Pain is not necessarily bad, and pleasure is not necessarily good. Though certain religious dogmas have unwisely taught us that we are degraded by partaking of Life's feast; and that we become holier by whipping ourselves, this is but un-wisdom. It all depends on our perception of what simply is. Our thoughts alone define what we consider to be a reward or a punishment, though both are equally valuable lessons from our Creator. These lessons guide us upward on the golden pathway of evolution.

Experiences of pain and pleasure must be equally served, to obtain balance and vitality. Muscles must be exercised consistently at their limit to achieve maximum growth. "No pain, no gain" has a certain validity. Use it or lose it.

When we Love the Light of Truth, it is reflected from us bright as a beacon to other seekers. We are here to learn to embrace both sides of Life. We cannot accumulate a great quantity of one side of wealth without the other side. Every coin must have a heads and a tails!

XIV

BAD AND GOOD

"Bad" and "good" are measure marks on the same ruler. A stone rolling down a hill will continue downward. A cloud rising upward will continue up. Is the one good, and the other bad? Similarly, like begets like through momentum. Remember the car? Thoughts moving away from Divine order are increasingly chaotic over time and distance, introducing elements of disorder to our lives. Thoughts moving toward Love enjoy stability and calm, as one nears the center of Being. A hurricane is turbulent at its rim, while peaceful in its eye. Both conditions exist simultaneously. We choose the direction we travel, in or out of the storm.

Our perceptions of "good" and "bad" are arbitrary. Illusion often leads us to believe that we can plant corn and expect wheat, but it is not so. Good and bad are distorted interpretations of what is, in Life. Divinity is the seed of Truth, filled with perfection, order, and Love, planted by Soul, and nourished by conscious effort with gratitude for our Creator, resulting in Divine action. An Olympic athlete trains body, mind, and spirit for a lifetime, in quest of a single victorious moment. Inspired thought and wise action guide us to the center, the winner's circle. Bad and good are but the necessary training steps along the journey.

Divinity is the seed of Truth, filled with perfection, order, and Love, planted by Soul, and nourished by conscious effort with gratitude for our Creator, resulting in Divine action.

XXV

SUFFERING

Our sense of true self-worth is the natural product of Love and gratitude for Divine order. In contrast, the drive for materialism without spiritual-ism, compels a lingering need for hard countable wealth; its luxury and enjoyment always seems to be offset by the calculation, "Is this enough now?" In frustration, the answer is usually no, unless we learn to think and grow inwardly wealthy through peace of mind.

Capitalism is justifiably designed to be self-perpetuating; by encouraging consumers to seek perpetual gratification for emotional or physical needs, wants, and desires which never can be fully satisfied. Though material worth conveys no permanent contentment, it is extremely useful in allowing us the privilege to seek these goals in more refined arenas. It frees us to enter a larger toy store. Money is a physical symbol of an energy concept. Like electricity, money is neither bad nor good; money will be what we will it to be.

Once again, we must pass through the gates of illusion of the outer world, to attain mastery of the inner world. The Master can be with and be without equally.

May we commit ourselves to the fulfillment of our purpose in Life in spite of external conditions. May we learn to love beyond attachments or addictions. May we remain centered and not swayed by anything, which pulls us off to one side or the other, or pushes us mentally off balance. Walking the straight and narrow line, like walking a fence or tightrope, is difficult at first; but the faster we walk, the easier it gets (due to the Law of Momentum), and the more quickly we reach our destination.

Our experiences are tests on the path of Divine evolution. To have and have not is a test. To be humble or proud is a test. To be thankful or not thankful is a test. Even prayer itself is a test of our understanding Universal Law. For instance, prayer is not to be a by-product of distress, to be pulled out of our trunk in an emergency like a spare tire. True prayer is not, "Oh God, please help me." True prayer is, "Thank you, God. I understand now that you are already helping me."

It may be difficult at times to thank God for seemingly unanswered prayers; but all true prayer sets unseen higher forces in motion, whose directions will become obvious weeks, months, or even years later. Never doubt this, for it is called wisdom. "Fear is an absence of wisdom, and wisdom is an absence of Fear." Our test in times of trouble, when we see only one set of footprints in the sand, is whether we think we are alone, or whether we know that God is carrying us. True prayer has true worth. Prayer is always answered with that special wisdom which aligns us powerfully with our Universe. Love conquers all.

XXVI

JUSTICE

Perfect justice reigns in a perfect, balanced Universe; and our Soul knows that every action shall meet inevitably with an equivalent reaction. The concept of "dysfunction" is erroneous, for it necessarily implies the imperfection of an orderly universe. Everything always balances. No mortal can improve upon the Law of Divine balance, though many have tried.

We live in harmony to the extent that we appreciate harmony. A higher Judge sits at the bench, to free us from the need to evaluate every action of our fellow travelers on the planet. Which part of our body deserves more blood as a reward for its special service?

Ultimately, we only perceive ourselves reaping injustice when we judge others. Fickle society condemns behavior one day and embraces it the next. Witness, for example, "The Sexual Revolution," in which many previous rules of conduct were overturned in favor of "Free Love." Of course, nothing is free, and you get what you pay for. Society reaps its own seed, and there are unforeseen penalties to such roller coaster behavior, as the outer world cycles through its inevitable peaks and decays of so-called "morality." How much greater is that Life designed for Universal order to triumph! That which is mortal perishes, rises and falls like dust in the wind. That which aligns with Love and Law parallels the forces of Immortality. We are alive as long as we are Love. We are to love as long as we live.

XXVII

MIRACLE VERSUS LAW

As every musician knows, a musical instrument has a range of notes it can play (actually vibrations of air we call "sound"), from lower to higher. A piano is able to sing eighty-eight tones from its keys, and infinity of melodies. A rainbow similarly has a range of colors, which are vibrations of light, from low (infra-red) to high (ultra-violet). Sound and Light are the stuff of which everything is made: vibrations of energy in time and space. "And God *Said*, 'Let there be *Light*."

Many mysteries exist which are invisible to us, unless we have a way to be initiated into their presence. Transparent electro-magnetic waves fly through the ether unseen, until the right magic box translates their essence back to its original substance: music, speech, and moving pictures. We call the magic boxes "radio" and "television." We push buttons and speak to a family member thousands of miles away, unaware of the dancing electrons in our "telephone." We swallow a few small capsules to chase away illnesses, which have killed millions of people in times past, and are annoyed by the heavy traffic on our way to the drug store. It is a "miracle" only to the uninitiated, for we are surrounded by such miracles every day.

How quickly we take miracles for granted, once the novelty wears off. In the Dark Ages, one of us could have probably ruled the world with a common flashlight...at least until the batteries ran down.

All vibrations are assigned "octaves" (do-re-mi-fa-so-la-ti-do) which define their specific rank in the hierarchy between zero and infinity. Lower octaves resonate to base materialism and the illusion of imbalance. Higher octaves are the playground of pure thought, Truth, Gratitude, and Love. We have control over our perception of lower vibrations in our physical realm of illusion, while our Soul is guardian of our Higher, more vibrant Self.

There exists a hierarchy of octaves guided by our Soul. Truth has its own octave. Love has its own octave. Gratitude has its own octave. Our physical plane also has its hierarchy. Gold and diamonds ascend a ritual of purification by fire; and so do human beings. Illusion adds color to that which is colorless. A pure diamond has the least color and the most fire.

Illusions affect our health, our spirituality, our career, our finances, our friends, and our family. Success in every area is a direct reflection of our dominant thought, as the full moon reflects the sun. But the moon also has a dark side. We are free to choose either face. If we listen to our illusions, we receive the profane. We stand before the temple, to be blown away with the sand. If we listen to our Soul, we build the temple and we become the sacred.

All that which is mortal is not immortal. That which is not directly in line with our purpose will crumble like the walls of Jericho. Everyone will be famous for fifteen minutes; but look around you and ask, "What has survived 2,000 years?" The mortal perishes, the immortal reigns.

Many mysteries exist which are invisible to us, unless we have a way to be initiated into their presence.

XXVIII

BEAUTIFUL THOUGHTS

Service performed with Love is a direct expression of our magnificent Universe. We live in the Divine exactly to the degree we express the Divine. Who can we blame if we dip into the fountain of Divine abundance with a thimble? Wisdom is a precursor to true loving service, for we know intuitively that we can give joyfully from an infinite fountain of wealth. It is all God's money...we just write and cash the checks.

Beautiful thoughts blended with faith act like key action steps toward genuine success. True achievement is possible only when we become aligned with true Power, true Wisdom and true Love. These elements build the magic carpet that we may ride to our dreams.

If we choose to deny this Truth, Universal Intelligence will be quick to point out the illusions of our ways. Pain, turmoil, insanity, infatuation, resentment, excess, deficiency, disease, all result from denying simple Laws of balance and harmony, refusing to recognize or admit the perfection of a perfect Universe.

A few of the secrets of Life are; to acknowledge the magnificence of our creation; to appreciate the philosophy ("philos"- loving, "sophy"- wisdom) of Divine order; and to see with eyes of balance. We are given our two eyes so that we can see both sides, and our one heart for the higher reason of our Soul. If we begin to see the beauty, beyond the immediate beauties of our eyes, we will unconditionally appreciate this beauty in all places, throughout all times. From a universal distance, everything is beautiful.

Our Universe is a magnificent expression of the Divine; any other interpretation is illusive, and will ultimately collapse under its own weight. We become part of this perfection precisely to the extent that we align ourselves powerfully with Divine Love and Divine Law. Human nature tends to seek "the easy way out." This often becomes the hardest road to travel, for an "easy" path also walks against the wind, instead of with it. There is no such thing as something for nothing, and Universal Law will always find a way to balance its books. Fortunately, all roads eventually lead to God, if we simply follow our heart's wise direction. A philo-sopher sat in the great Muslim temple of the Kabba, with his feet toward the sacred stone instead of his head.   When chastised for this apparent blasphemy, he replied, "You tell me where God is not, and I will put my feet there." God is felt in every atom, every living creature, every leaf, and every cosmos. We stand in awe with unfolding awareness of God omnipotent, God omniscient, God omnipresent. A father and mother will raise their child with compassion and understanding, in the hope that these qualities of their example shall become part of the child too. So it is with infinite expression of God through us. This is the Love of God for us.

XXIX

WILL AND PURPOSE
WITH THANKS

Our thoughts can be either mortal or immortal. Mortal thoughts breed desperation. Immortal thoughts birth inspiration. Desperate thoughts mold obstacles; inspired thoughts melt them.

Our true purpose in Life is to love and to lift and inspire those around us, through the loving of that which is within us. We Love the outer world only so far as we Love the inner world. We Love the inner world only to the extent that we can Love the outer world. We Love ourselves only as much as we Love others. Life is a reflection of us. Do we Love what we see in the mirror?

Our conscious Being seeks permission to Love, for it knows intuitively that Love casts out fear, calms every storm, wins every victory. It is said that we are never alone as long as someone, somewhere loves us and as long as we love.

When we listen to the Light of our Soul we have gratitude and love for our magnificent Universe. We realize that every obstacle simply reminds us to release our heart bow, which shoots out flowering arrows of thanks. Our bow will allow us to shoot our loving arrows, toward the dreams we truly love. An obstacle is clearly our misunderstanding of what magnificence there is. Life is a movie screen; it will reflect whatever we project upon it. Every loving dream, every loving wish is possible. We simply must awaken to the purpose for which we came.

Our conscious Being seeks permission to Love, for it knows intuitively that Love casts out fear, calms every storm, wins every victory.

Dr. John F. Demartini

XXX

BODY LANGUAGE

Our outer appearance is an expression of our inner thoughts. Our body speaks its own language. Our eyes are the windows of our Soul. Our physical body is a great gift from our Creator. Our form uses the brain to process lessons of Love. Its biochemical essence is transmitted to every cell of our being. Each cell contains the vibration of our thoughts, just as every drop of water in the ocean is the ocean. We give more respect to our physical form as we learn to Love, for it is the temporary vehicle which helps carry us to our destination. Many of us pay more attention to our cars than we do for our wellness; and which of us want a car that is neglected, running on cheap fuel, and always breaking down?

Our body maintains harmony in its structure as we learn to respect it, through recognition of our intrinsic perfection. If we do not learn to Love it, we literally get in our own way, blocking the flow of Life force to our body's tissues and organs. "Dis-ease" is a lack of easy access of our Life energy to some

88

area of our body. "I can't stomach this..." "I can't swallow that..." "I can't stand this..." "Don't hand me that..." or the classic, "This is killing me!" are all verbal expressions of subconscious cries for love. When we have such thoughts we end up with stomach problems, sore throats, leg and foot pain, numb hands, or even the belief that we don't deserve to physically live.

We may cut off the circulation of energy, or swell it beyond its intended capacity. Both are evidence of our dis-harmony in the mental realm, distress, which has worked its way down to the physical structure, like rain through a hole in the roof. As above, so below.

"Wellness" on the other hand is a natural combination of vitality and balance. When vitality and balance are restored, spontaneous healing occurs. Some people call this sudden restoration of health a "miracle," but our health is a natural product of perfect alignment with our Soul.

Our physical form can be compared to a computer screen: it processes and displays what is going on with the program, without being the program. Our thought processes running inside us combine software (such as genetic patterns and experiences after birth) with hardware (bones, muscle, lung capacity) and firmware (that which we can consciously and willfully modify, such as the intentional pursuit of self-evolvement and wellness).

Spontaneous healing takes place when we follow wise actions and listen to the Light of our Soul. Miracle after miracle after miracle is possible to all human beings the moment they acknowledge the magnificence of creation, with gratitude and Love. All we must do is seize the Divine Wisdom available to us. Life is as love filled as we allow it to be.

When vitality and balance are restored, spontaneous healing occurs. Some people call this sudden restoration of health a "miracle," but our health is a natural product of perfect alignment with our Soul.

XXXI

BODY LANGUAGE II

Illness, disease, or disorder is a perceived absence of wellness, health or order. Illness is a loss of potential vitality and balance. We become more aware of our physical body's presence through pain, aching joints, fatigue, sore muscles, internal organs, which is not playing in concert with the rest of the orchestra. Illness is a genuine blockage of energy, like a gentle but insistent stream, which must flow freely, or else burst its borders. The roots of illness are tangled in illusion, grasped by lies of imperfection.

Wellness, health, or order is a perceived absence of disease, illness or disorder. When we are well we simply ARE. When we ARE, we are filled with love and wisdom. Truth brings Wisdom, which opens blocked channels and allows a natural free flow of energy to and from all parts of the body. Wisdom is healing; it is the Light of our Soul radiated through the Love and gratitude of our heart. It is the most powerful of all healers.

Illusion wants to keep our instrument out of tune, lead us down a path of sensual craving, by drawing us to fleeting attractions, improper diet, inadequate exercise, and other "easy" ways out; easy at least until we end up in the hospital, worn out before our time, mentally disturbed, or visiting an early grave. The physical body is an instrument to teach us Love. It functions perfectly when we learn to Love it, for our body is the temple, the vessel for Divine essence. Love is tears of inspiration, music to our ears, and a meaningful sight for sore eyes. Love heals.

Wisdom is healing; it is the Light of our Soul radiated through the Love and gratitude of our heart. It is the most powerful of all healers.

XXXII

FOOD FOR THOUGHT

It is said that our eyes are the windows of our Soul. If this is so, then our physical bodies are its houses. Our Soul is our physician, our minister, our teacher; its presence enters the very fiber of our being. Our dominant thought affirms or denies the authority we entrust to our Soul's higher authority in our lives. If our thought is positive or negative, it shows in our face like a television screen. If our thoughts are repeated persistently over time, their effects will become stamped on our body, positive or negative. As above, so below.

The moon reflects a predictable, indelible lunar cycle every twenty-eight days, ranging from full darkness to full brilliance. The "lunatic" also has a cycle, running from depression to mania and back again to depression. In illusion, we fall prey to lunatic cycles of emotion, rage followed by remorse, bouts of physical instability (such as under- and over-eating), cycles of imbalance where too little of this demands too much of that. These are signs that we are running as fast as we can and getting nowhere, like a hamster on its wheel. Cycles always take us back near to where we started, even if we don't want to be there. Shades of cyclical behavior reflect in our face like shadows of the moon.

Emotion is based in untruth, imagined imperfection in that which simply is. In broader terms, we have what IS, and then we have our stories about what IS. "Stories" are very similar to ancient folklore: they change every time we tell them. Details get added, a little flourish here, a small exaggeration there, until the legend assumes a life of its own. Stories are hard to defend when asked the question, "How do you know?"

Our Story is almost always subjective, very opinionated, possibly misleading, and often completely untrue, yet it can cause a lifetime of illusive hardships and 'grief', as if we have convicted ourselves and sent ourselves to jail for a crime we did not commit. There is no mistaking the hardened eyes, the hardened face, and the hardened heart of one whose thoughts are hard. We are free only when we let ourselves out of jail.

Love warms and smoothes cold edges, softens our eyes with tears of inspiration, removes the chains of steel around our hearts, lights our faces with a shining radiance for everyone to see. All Life secretly yearns to reach the Sun, with its beckoning eternal Light. There is no darkness at the Sun, no cycle of day or night, summer or winter. The sun simply is. Wisdom centers its attention on this Light. God is Light.

Dr. John F. Demartini

Love warms and smoothes cold edges, softens our eyes with tears of inspiration, removes the chains of steel around our hearts, lights our faces with a shining radiance for everyone to see.

XXXIII

DEFINITENESS OF PURPOSE

Definiteness of purpose is the clearest and brightest road to success in any endeavor. If you don't know where you are going, you will probably end up somewhere else.

We attune to or arrive on this planet with a purpose. Our calling in life, if we choose to accept it, is to discover this purpose, and fulfill it. In fulfilling our purpose, we become aligned with Universal power, which naturally wants us to succeed on our mission. After all, the Universe is the best-run business "in the Universe".

Our thoughts crystallize in purity as we attune to higher frequencies, greater concentric spheres of Truth, and more brilliant intensities of Light. The way to see the Light is to be the Light. We attract people, places, ideas, and events, which coincide with our intent. We become clear and certain, when our guiding Light is expressing its clarity and certainty.

If we build walls to block this beacon, through ignorance, fear, or uncertainty, then we are truly adrift in the darkness, without direction, upon a turbulent sea with many rocks. We automatically stop our progress if we cut ourselves off from our Light. This is a method of physical self-destruction, for that which is finite must return to dust. God is Light, God is Truth, and therefore Light is Truth. Earth is constantly bathed in Light, and each light particle carries a grain of immortal Truth, waiting patiently for us to open our eyes and see it, open our hearts and be it.

We wear our human forms like a suit of clothes. This is why our appearance changes so dramatically over years from child to adult, or in seconds from frown to smile. Even our body language changes its vocabulary. We can evolve our lives miraculously when we understand this principle.

Appearance is illusion, as every actor and actress knows, for the entire world's a stage. Trompe l'oeil, fool the eye is the rule in illusion. All that glitters is not gold. If our dominant thought is chained to our appearance, then it will perish with our form, as a plant dies without water or nourishment. If we listen to doubts about our physical bodies, we perceive ourselves as transient, growing old, running in fear, wandering in catastrophe, guilt and anxiety.

When we listen to the particles of Truth constantly bombarding us, waiting patiently for us, we dictate our destiny as a star in the making. Our immortal nature blooms. We walk the path of stars. When we see ourselves as Light, an expression of Divinity, our purpose shines. We become Stars.

Earth is constantly bathed in Light, and each light particle carries a grain of immortal Truth, waiting patiently for us to open our eyes and see it, open our hearts and be it.

XXXIV

TIME

Blessed is that fortunate individual who has a definite purpose in Life, who has a big enough "Why?" If purpose grows from Love, the "How" will reveal itself.

The greatest action is purposeful action. The greatest cause is purposeful cause. If we open our heart, obey its wish then all Law is at our command. Success is inevitable, though the path may be steep and the eagle's talons sharp, for the Universe wants us to succeed.

Time is a precious commodity. There are always two straight paths from Point A to Point B on this planet. One is the short straight road; the other is the long straight road. "He went straight home, but he took the long way...around the world." The difference is that something perceived as time.

If we wander around in physical sensory illusion, aimless and pointless, distractions will precipitate into our lives. Time is the coin of this realm. Its savings of a lifetime are deposited into our bank account in advance. We may squander it uselessly in pursuit of sensory gratification; or we can align with the immortal and reap all conceivable treasure. We are the potential masters of all we survey. Life is urgent.

Purpose unfolds genius, unleashes inspiration and fires the imagination. When we are on fire, the crowd comes to watch us burn.

Consistent daily purpose is learning to walk the walk and talk the talk, until it is such a natural part of us that we become our vision and verbal expression. Each great achievement starts with a single great thought, combined with definite purposeful action, and the unshakeable belief that we will fulfill in the end. Thomas Edison: "I had to succeed; I ran out of things which didn't work." The sharper our focus, the clearer our vision, the better we can see where we are going.

Persistence through the winter enables a tree to grow new leaves in springtime. As surely as night follows day, we will experience difficult times in pursuit of ease; but the wise student remembers there are cycles to every season, and Nature has dictated that spring always follows winter. It is our destiny to persist, to stay on course with a definite purpose. It is said that we came to master love here... and some of us who stay will learn very well indeed.

The lives of mortals are filled with irregular fragments, like scattered pieces of a picture puzzle whose whole image they can never see. Mastery brings immortal membership in a Divine order where the whole is greater than the sum of its pieces. Divine order is The Big Picture. All Masters of art, literature, science, business, and every creative endeavor use persistence with definiteness of purpose and belief in their ultimate victory, to achieve their goals and reach their immortal destiny. Their Soul calls to them, drives them gently yet irresistibly, until success is won. Our Soul is calling us. Now!

XXXV

DISCIPLINE AND EFFICIENCY

A tree demonstrates perfect balance between its branches and roots, or else it would topple over. A tree is a physical manifestation of a spiritual form: there is as much beneath the surface as above it. As above, so below. In fact, we can view this structure as two trees, one positive, one negative, each tree drawing nourishment and sustenance from its own unique environment; complementary sources of basic elements all supporting each other for the mutual benefit and growth of both trees. (In this case: rain, soil, air, and sunlight or water, earth, wind and fire.)

We are also trees. Our roots are planted in Soul, our purpose in life forms the trunk, which in turn supports the branches, which grow the fruits of our labor. This fruit may be given freely to our neighbors; we might hoard it; or it may simply fall to the ground and rot. We must listen to our Soul, so that we shall hear of its intent for our fruit. Wisdom fuels our roots, builds our tree, which reaches toward the sun, offers our blessings to the cornucopia of Humanity, so all can partake of the feast.

We show "discipline," we become "disciples" when we listen to our Soul and follow our purpose. Definiteness of purpose defines wise action, for it directs us on the straight, short path to our destination. We exhibit high-priority thoughts, high-priority actions which efficiently direct our talents to our fulfillment of purpose. Our highest priority is hearing the wisdom of our Soul, seeing the light of our Soul, and following the direction of our Soul. By listening to our "still small voice," by seeing our inner vision consistently, we affirm wise action and we feel our heart filled with flowers of love. Focus, focus, focus, and more focus. Like a magnifying glass, our vision becomes sharper, our heat more intense. We develop the qualities of a master day by day, through exercising our potential, just as an athlete builds muscle and coordination with persistent effort over time. We learn to be a V.I.P. or a Very Important Person with Vitality Intensity and Power and with Vision Inspiration and Purpose.

Effective Life is purpose and action. Every cell of our being knows its purpose, and what it is designed to do. There is no confusion. The picture becomes cloudy only when we start to think how we would run the show if we were king of the world, instead of allowing our Soul to guide and direct us. We drift into lives of quiet desperation punctuated with emotional gunfire when the pressure of our illusion explodes us. "Living" is different from "Life." "Living" is an aimless wandering in the desert of our senses, reacting to our surroundings like beasts, looking for the next oasis in a hostile environment, dallying briefly just long enough to ask, "Is that all there is?" and restlessly moving on, searching endlessly for Paradise and the meaning of Life. "Life," on the other hand, is definite purpose with definite action, moving in a definite direction, guided by Soul, flying to the stars with the angels.

Our highest priority is hearing the wisdom of our Soul, seeing the light of our Soul, and following the direction of our Soul.

XXXVI

ACHIEVEMENT

Our vanity imagines that our so-called failings are due to some external unbeatable force, rather than some personal internal 'weakness' of character. The arena of illusion promotes an exciting spectacle of endless battle, us against the world, where someone is always doing something to us. In reality, there is no separation between seer, seeing, and scenery. All are One, seamlessly integrated as a whole. Perception of gain or loss is an illusion, for these occur only in the shifting sand of our minds. Actually, everything this planet started with is still here, whether it was an atom, a grain of sand or a chunk of gold. All exists in perpetual symmetry, only the form changes. A diamond is fused carbon in disguise, little more than a well-mannered lump of coal. Yet the diamond obtained its form over thousands of years through integration with its surroundings, definiteness of purpose with wise action to produce an object of beauty. A raw diamond needs only to be polished to show its brilliance. We have that same opportunity.

Poise is the art of simply Being, to be in the world without being of the world. Equal poise is Truth revealed. Unequal poise is poison.

Seek poise. Focus on poise whatever the circum-stance. Understand that true justice, true law, true order, always reigns. Our transient misinterpretation of events may contradict this; but no mortal has the power to interfere with genuine poise. Poise is the realm of the gods themselves, free from the turbulent winds of illusion.

This simple truth is not in the hands of the many though it is in their hearts all along. They allow themselves to be tossed around like driftwood on the ocean. This same piece of driftwood could be carved, through diligent effort, into a boat with rudder and oars, a vessel to carry us toward our destiny. Of course there is more driftwood than sailing ships, for that with the least value circulates the most. It is "easier" to go with the flow, rather than think and act as an individual. This is evident on every level, for popular ideas and belief systems often have the least value. A basic tenet of business is to see what the majority is doing, then do just the opposite, for the majority are invariably unwise. Everyone would be rich if being rich was easy.

Masters seek Truth in spite of superficial appearance. Truth withstands the test of time. We awaken gradually into perpetual Light, the Light, which remains intense whether or not we have our eyes, shut. Little children close their eyes, and imagine themselves powerful because the stars disappear. But Truth awaits perpetually in our heart. Truth is Love.

XXXVII

SACRIFICE

How do we sacrifice to God, when everything already belongs to God? We may present a symbolic offering of our labor, affection, fear, or need. This symbol itself represents a personal concept of sacrifice. A mother takes food from her own lips to feed a hungry child. But God is not hungry. A wealthy matron places her diamond ring in the church collection plate. But God made the diamond and the gold.

We can make only one genuine sacrifice: to forsake our illusions and unite with God through Soul. Superstition believes that pleasure or wrath from heaven is provoked by external tokens. Leaders of opposing armies each proclaim before battle, "God is on our side." But godhood, godly affairs, godly favors are above such tests. The sacred temple of Truth is revealed when Humanity sacrifices its plunder and blunder. We sacrifice our mortal self; we stand at the altar, and rid us of that which we do not want: deceit about our Universe, lies about our Being, stories about the world around us, imagined flaws in that which is perfect.

Let us acknowledge truth with gratitude and enter the temple of Life. Let us become an immortal expression of Divine Light in physical form. Let a Heart of gold pour its ambrosia of Love into every one of our vessels, and accept our purposeful destinies willingly. Let us walk through the darkened doorway where fear lurks and actively turn on the light of true sacrifice. Let us walk the path. Let us take reactions and put them into actions. Let us find the balance of every imbalanced illusion. Let us ask ourselves in a humble manner where we may perceive such illusions. Let us accept cause and effect and then we have sacrificed. Let us analyze ourselves and look deeply, because whatever we see in others is us. Whatever we see in the world around us is us. When we love the things around us, we find the Love within us. Now we have sacrificed. Now we are ready and we have initiated ourselves. We are no longer neophytes. We are now Adepts, standing at the sacred temple in humble Soulfullness expressing our Truth. Now we 'deserve' the Light of God.

Let us acknowledge truth with gratitude and enter the temple of Life. Let us become an immortal expression of Divine Light in physical form. Let a Heart of gold pour its ambrosia of Love into every one of our vessels, and accept our purposeful destinies willingly.

XXVIII

THE GOLDEN THREAD
OF TRUTH

We cannot put our hands into a pot of glue without some of the glue sticking. Similarly, we cannot put our thoughts into the dominant thoughts of great Immortals without their thoughts sticking with us. We will see the scenery of immortality if we walk the path of nobility with our eyes open, because our Soul lights our way.

Let us release sensation, judgment, prejudice, bias, distorted perception, invalid systems of illusion. Let us cease to be ruled by opinions, that intoxicating bane of society at large. Society is many followers looking for one leader. Let us allow Truth, Purity, Light, Life, Love, Wisdom, and Power to enter. These qualities automatically confer nobility and immortality.

Love withstands the test of time. If we unify our heart with action, allow our voice to sing in harmony with Life we endure. There are two kinds of people in this world: people who are looking for God, and people who have found God, mortals and immortals. May we sew with the golden thread of truth.

XXXIX

DREAMS

We live in the present. Indeed it is a present, a gift to be treasured. We come here with a purpose, a void we are to fill, a yearning for completeness. Our insecurity stems from an imagined separation from divinity, as if we could somehow exist apart from this universe, like an extra gear in a fine Swiss watch. But what would be the purpose of an extra gear?

Our dreams reconnect us on a conscious level with Divinity. Dreams represent our ultimate values, a playground of the mind where anything is possible. It is the driving force of all greatness. A dream is a magic vine we can climb to a new plane of awareness, from where we can look down in safety at the struggle we have already overcome, at least in our thoughts. We can practice our words, perform our actions, imagine our calculations, design our monuments, and explore our farthest reaches of imagination. All that we conceive, we can achieve. Every "miracle" starts as a dream.

But dreaming is not for free, and we get what we pay for. There is no such thing as something for nothing in this Universe. We will not fulfill our dream unless we are willing to sacrifice our illusions. We must be able to hold onto *"de vine"* light of our Soul; pluck out any little weeds of consciousness which interfere with the strength of this vine.

Achievement is one percent inspiration, and ninety-nine percent perspiration. This is one measurable sacrifice of the mortal to the Immortal. May we have the wisdom and the discipline to listen to the light of our Soul and obey. By doing so, we sacrifice our outer form as a snake sheds its skin, a moth its cocoon, to spiral our way back to the Light of Life. We are baptized, cleansed, purified and reborn from death into Life. Our mortal becomes Immortal, our finite becomes infinite, our root becomes fruit, our earthly living becomes heavenly life.

May we have the wisdom and the discipline to listen to the light of our Soul and obey.

XL

REALITY

Merrily, merrily, merrily, merrily, Life is but a dream. The Creator dreamed...we have creation. The Creators and sub-Creators, the hierarchy within the Heavens, all dream. We are no different. We are an expression of dreams, in turn expressing dreams. When we master the mastery of dreams, we become creative. As masters of dreams we have the willingness to listen to the Lights of our Souls and dominate our thoughts, our visions, and our affirmations on our missions. Our efforts give effects. Our causes initiate our effects. We create a very individualized reality, and bring into actuality through definite action. We cannot obtain without our dreams. Without our dreams, we perish.

We are destined to have a dream. This is our purpose. It gives us a vision. It gives us a calling. Those who are inspired with a vision and calling have the dream manifested and expressed through time and space. When we lose our vision and calling, we perish. We self-destruct our forms. Any of us who do not follow our inspirations and intuitions are designed to automatically experience entropy and destruction. Our physical resources go back to the collective pool, to be put to wiser use somewhere else. But those of us who follow our inspirations and intuitions, to those lofty heights of the Heavens we came from, eventually we obtain the very essence of its source: Light, Life, Love, Wisdom and Power.

When we open up our Heart with the gratitude key, we listen to the light of our Soul. Our heart becomes permeated into the vision and auditory message of the brain. We become the dream in our Heart, we become inspired, we become fuel, we become called, and we need no more outside motivation. Our Souls simply call us. It simply makes us act. It simply helps us create. It simply attracts the people, places, things, ideas and events into our Life to manifest our dominant thought. It is the source of Life itself. It is the dream that comes true. It is the secret of Life. We are to never lose sight of our dreams. May we hold on to our dreams throughout our lives as our purposes unfold. May we see that everything in the drop of water becomes the ocean, while the ocean becomes the drop of water. The rain is but part of a cycle of creation from the great Creator to the form and back to the Creator.

Our destiny is to take the One and make it into many pieces, and then to turn the parts back into the One. Our dream is the vehicle back to its source. It is the essence of Life, and we must master that dream. It is our destiny and direction to do so. The secret of Life is to find what that dream is in our Heart and follow it, regardless of what the obstacles are; because when we follow it, we have the dream come true.

Dr. John F. Demartini

The secret of Life is to find what that dream is in our Heart and follow it, regardless of what the obstacles are; because when we follow it, we have the dream come true.

XLI

REALITY II

Let us wish upon a star, for there is a pot of gold at the end of the rainbow. The pot of gold is the light of our Soul. The rainbow is our reflection of emotions that we must master and unify into order, so the gold can be ours and we can walk the path of the rainbow. The sun is our gift because it is our guide. It gives us our rainbow. If we lose sight of the sun, we cannot see the rainbow to guide our path to the gold. It is our secret to hold that vision and that dream, because it is the sun.

We are the Light of our Soul. Our dream is the sun, and may that shining Light guide our own Light forever. If we follow its beacon, we become Immortal, we become geniuses, we act in wisdom, we have courage, we behave with virtue, we become Immortals on this planet. We are guides and shining Lights to all people; they come to watch us burn, and some stay for the feast.

When we give Light, we receive greater Light. We are the stewards of God, entrusted with an ever-greater abundance of resources as we prove our skill in management and self-control. To them who have much shall more be given.

The Light of the sun is just a stepping-stone to the Light of the galaxy, which is just a stepping-stone to the Light of the Universe, which is nothing more than a stepping-stone to that which is even greater. We eventually realize, in greater and greater hierarchies, that the Light of our Soul is simply a stepping-stone to the gateway of all heavens, the divine domain. Our dream is the key. It is the portal. It gives vision to the immortal. May we never lose that vision. May we never lose our dream. May we walk the path of that dream, and may we love and be grateful. That is the key to our dream. As we conceive and believe, so shall we achieve.

XLII

LOVE, WISDOM, AND POWER

Our wavering and wandering is a sign that we have lost the direction of our Soul. Steadiness, poise and uprightness, calmness, serenity and inner peace are the signs that our Soul reveals for our progress. Our heart, when it is closed, creates our storms. Our heart, when it is open, calms our ocean.

When we have ingratitude, we miss out on the magnificence of the Universe. We automatically see the wishing, the washing, the wavering, the turmoil and the illusion. We react. We get caught. We beat ourselves up. We beat others up. We get angry and we miss out on the magnificence that is there. The secret of Life is gratitude, which is the key that opens our heart and breeds our calmness. It allows our mind's ocean to be in such a glassy state, the sun glimmers so perfectly that we can see the sun without a ripple.

If we are wise, we wake up and we look back. We say, "It was there all the time." We realize that self-induced circumstances were shaping us. We look into our past with

127

new eyes, and see that we were a diamond in the rough. All we needed was skillful polishing. The events and people who made us angry were really our teachers, our stonecutters and our polishers. They really wanted us to shine.

Everyone is a diamond. Everything is polish. We are roughened by the illusion of imperfection. We are smoothed by the awareness of our Soul. Calmness and serenity arise from this wisdom.

Love all people and all events in your life. They are your teachers. Whether we are a wise man, wise woman, or wise child, let us sit still, sit in silence, sit in gratitude, sit in poise, sit in Love, and sit with tears of inspiration. Let us acknowledge the magnificence of our Universe and God. Let us use our gifts. Let us say each day:

"I am a Genius, and I apply my Wisdom.
I do what I Love and I Love what I do."
"Thank you God I love you."

ABOUT THE AUTHOR

In ancient times and cultures there existed individuals whose span of experience and study encompassed broad scopes of knowledge. They were once called 'Philosophers'. In our modern era where specialists reign and where the general 'man of letters' is left to educating the future specialists, there rarely occur those individuals who could truly be called modern day philosophers.

Dr. John F. Demartini is one of these rare and gifted individuals. His scope of experience and knowledge has encompassed the intricacies of cosmology, the mysteries of theology and the magical essence of clinical psychology and healing. He has researched the great classical writings of both the Orient and Occident and has synthesized the message of the great ancient and modern masters. As a writer, his volumes of writings have spanned most of the questions of life. As a teacher and speaker, he travels extensively, unveiling the ancient mysteries hidden in the very meaning of our modern existence. When he speaks, hearts open, minds become inspired and bodies become motivated into action. He has been quoted as saying that: "a genius is one who sees the vision and listens to the message of their soul, and obeys" He is an individual who believes and lives such a vision and message.

Dr. Demartini is the author of numerous books, including *'Count Your Blessings – The Healing Power of Gratitude and Love,'* originator of *'The Breakthrough Experience,'* and *'The Quantum Collapse Process'* and founder of the *Concourse of Wisdom School of Philosophy and Healing.*

Dr. John F. Demartini

2800 Post Oak Blvd suite 5250

Houston, Texas 77056

Ph: 713-850-1234 or 888-DEMARTINI

Fax: 713-850-9239

www.drdemartini.com

Certain gifted writers have the ability to open up the doorway to the Soul and to share their wondrous insights in immortal works such as "The Prophet" by Kahlil Gibran or James Allen's perennial classic "As A Man Thinketh".

Now a new Soul experience is available. This new book *The Wisdom of the Oracle* (the result of inspired meditation and experience) opens up the doorway to the heart and the Soul. A rare jewel of inspired writing, *The Wisdom of the Oracle* offers profound insights into our earthly and spiritual powers. It reveals the practical and the enlightened way to overcome the troubles and complexities of everyday life.

*"**Wisdom of the Oracle** is simple, powerful and deeply meaningful. It will certainly reach through and touch your heart and Soul."*

Dr. John F. Demartini is a writer, teacher, and philosopher. He travels the world sharing his heart opening messages with millions. Some of his other books include: *Count Your Blessings – The Healing Power of Gratitude and Love* and *Lessons for Life.* He is Founder of the *Concourse of Wisdom School of Philosophy and Healing.*

1st Books

Library™

www.1stBooks.com